THOMAS
CHURCHWELL
DOT COM

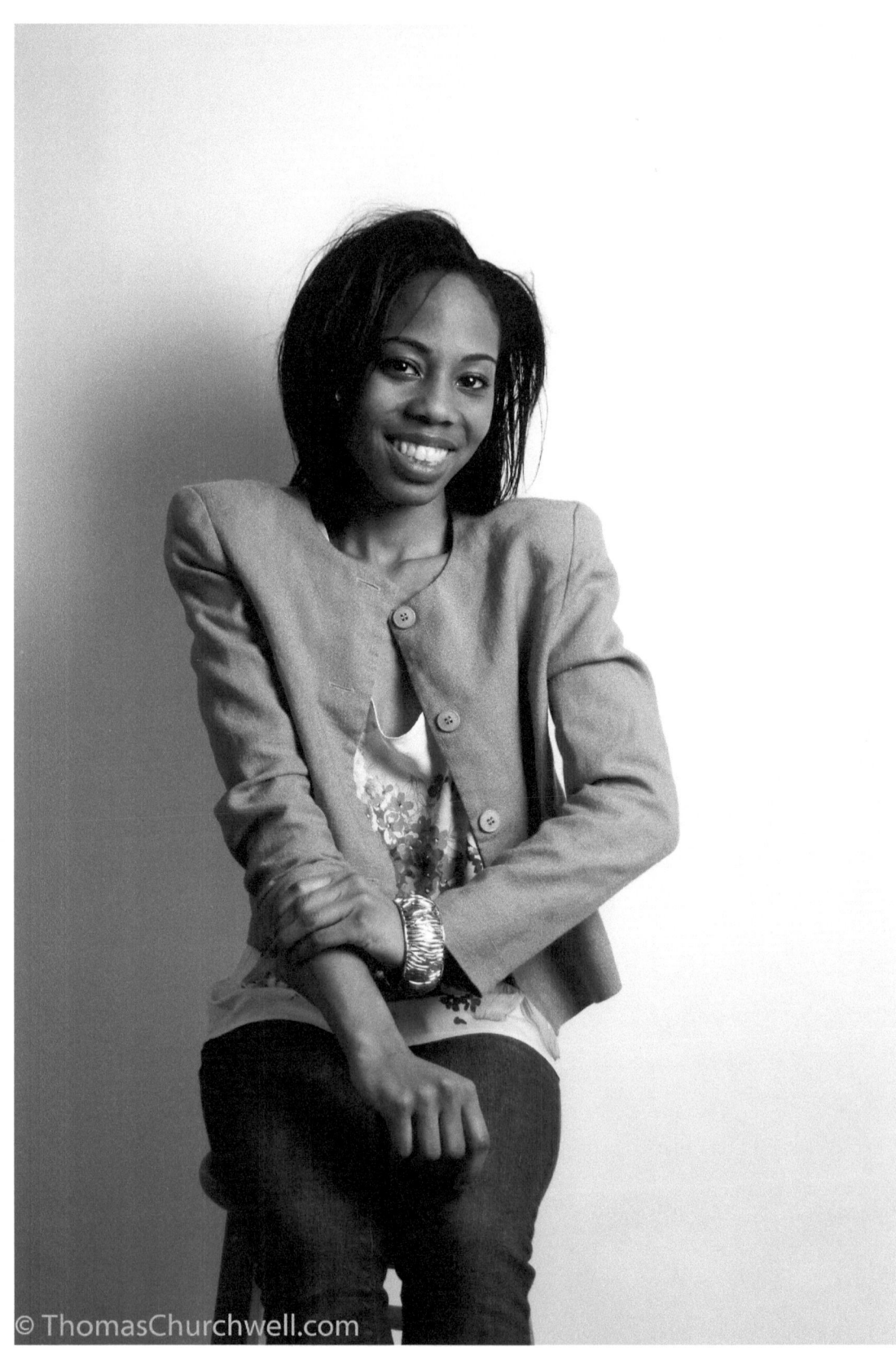

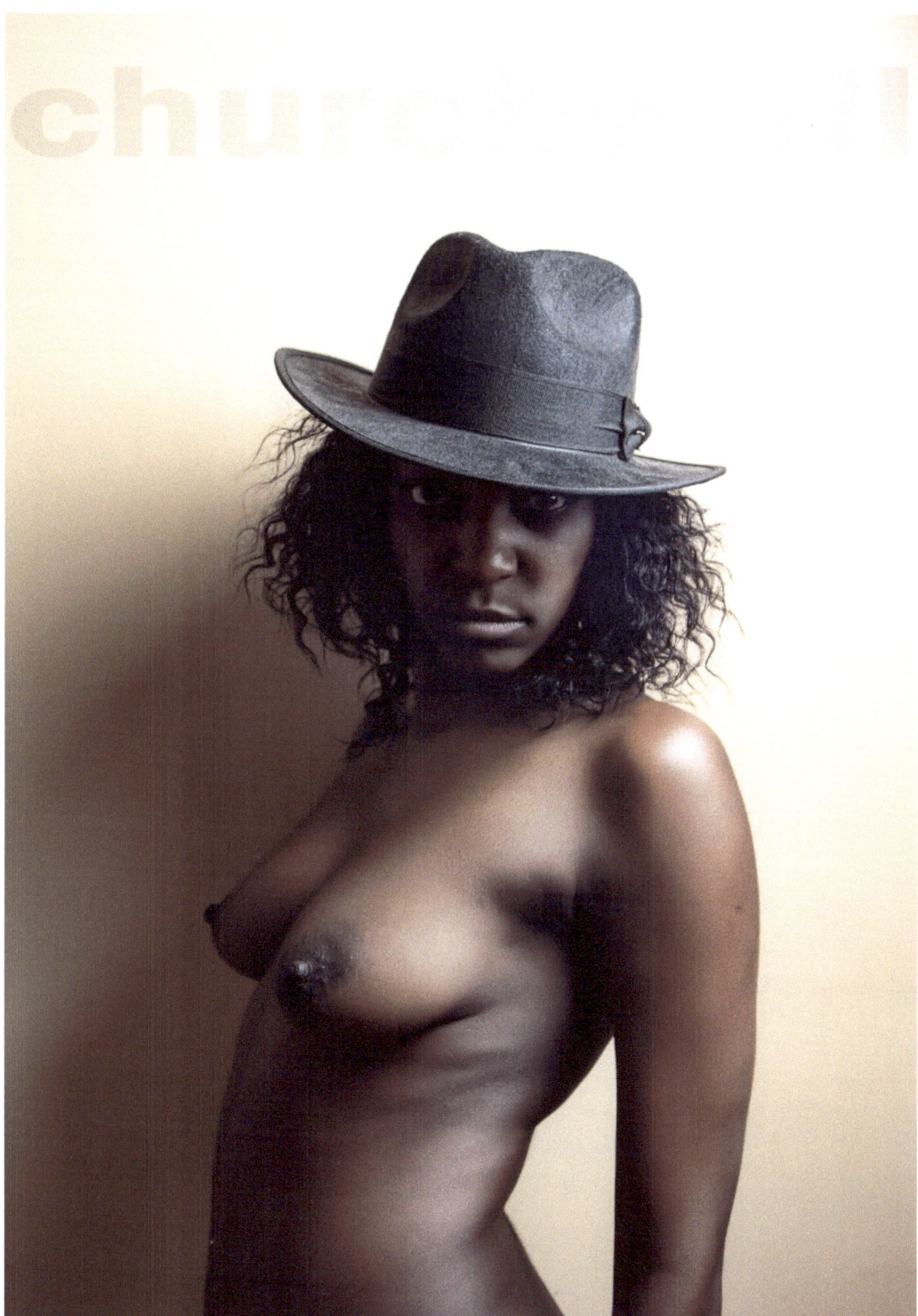

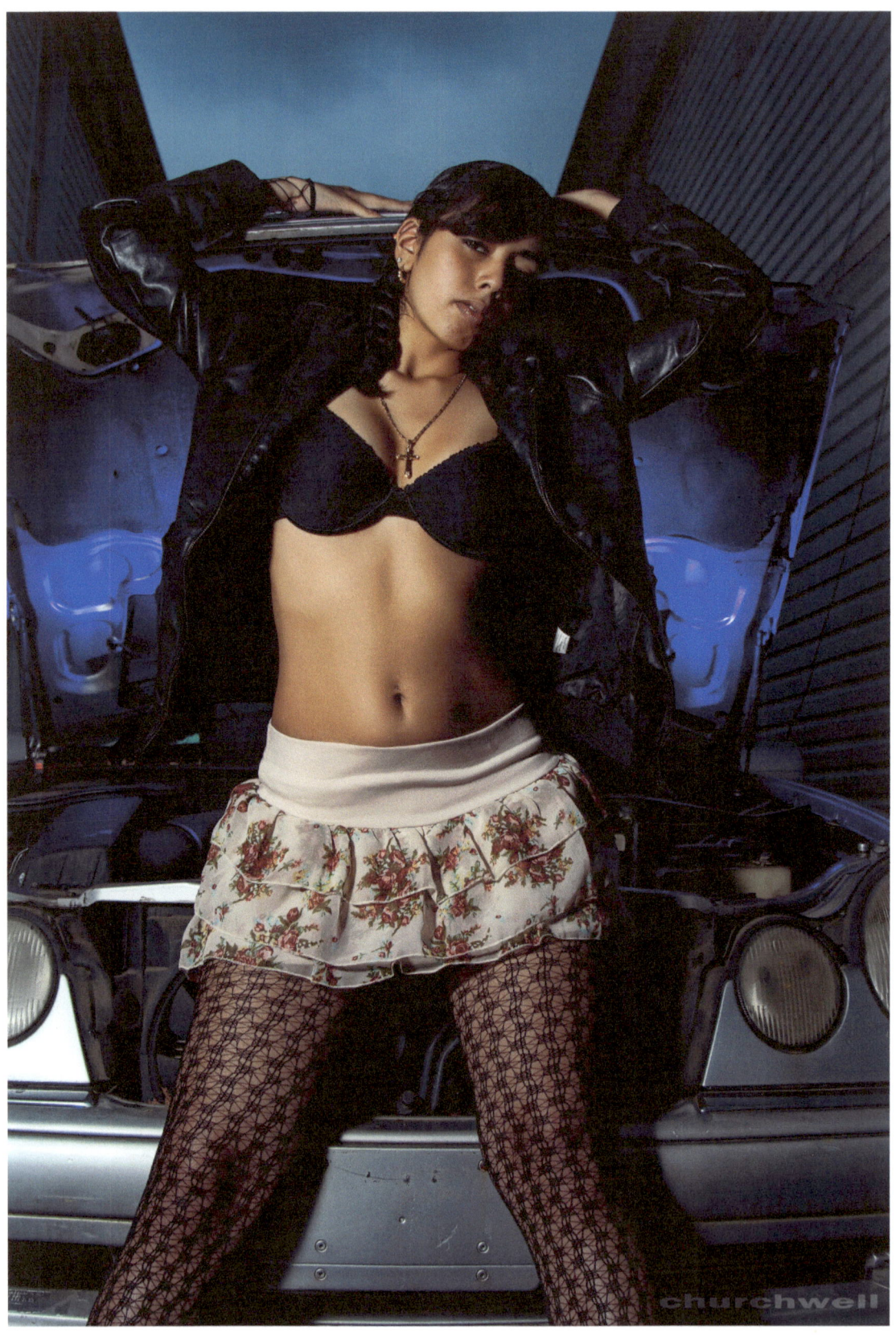

churchwell

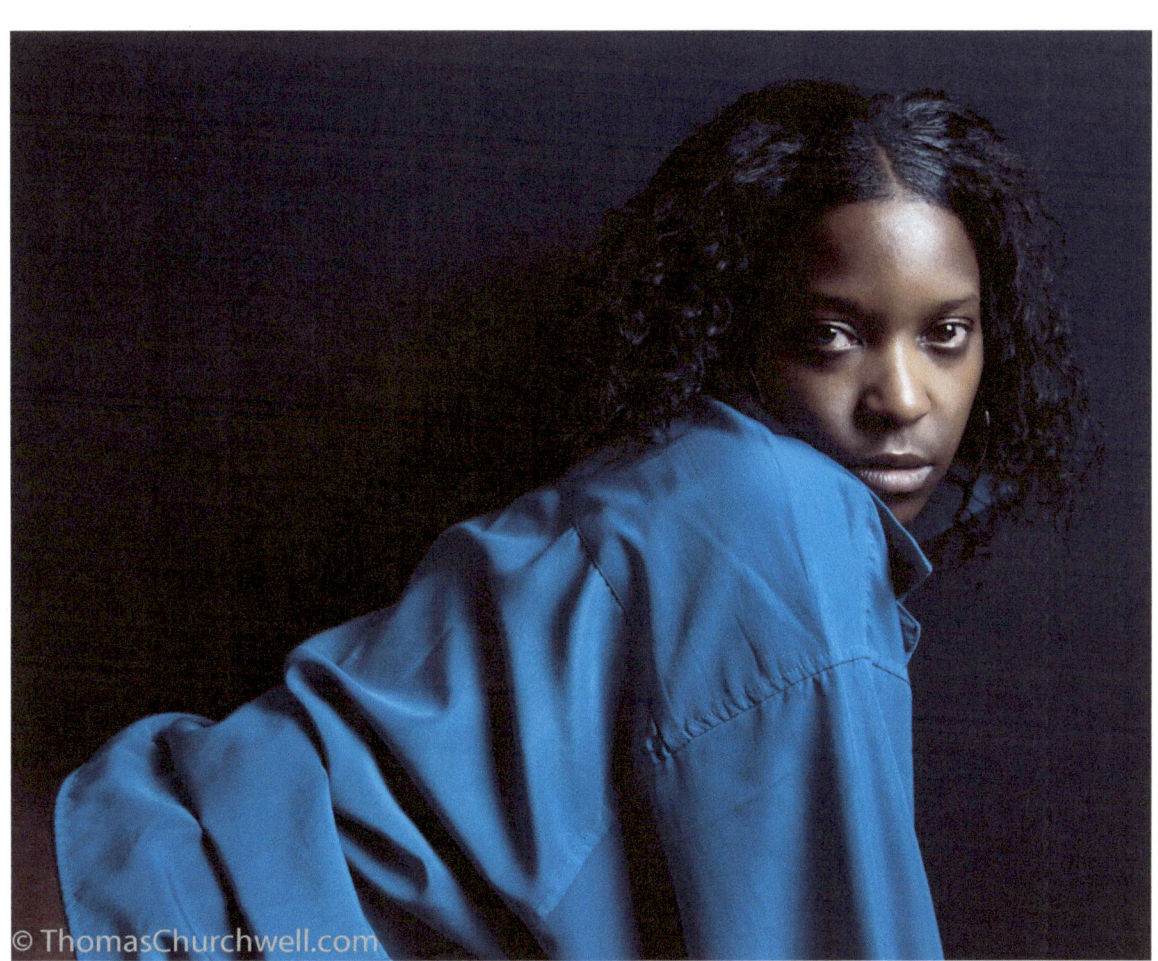

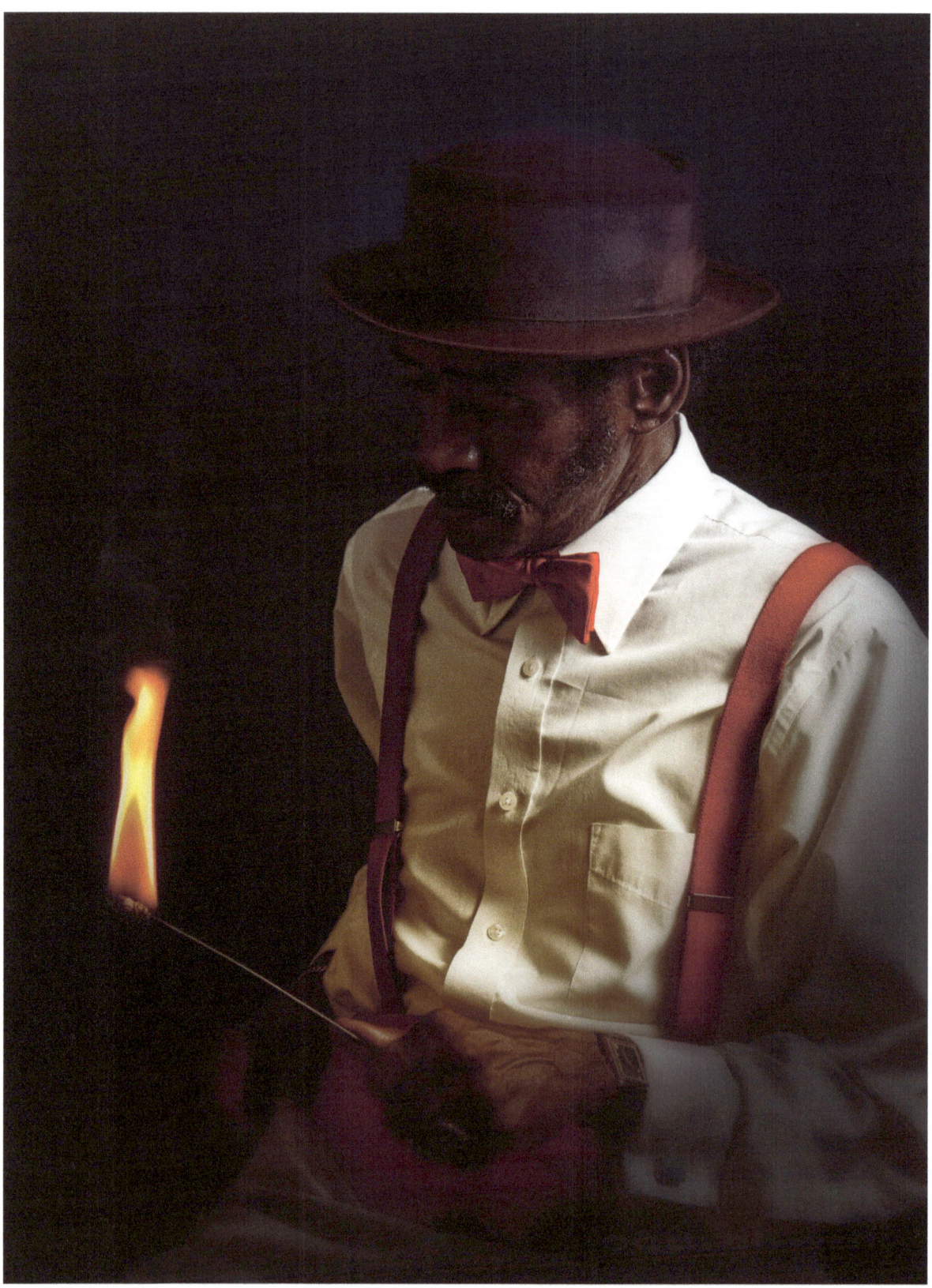

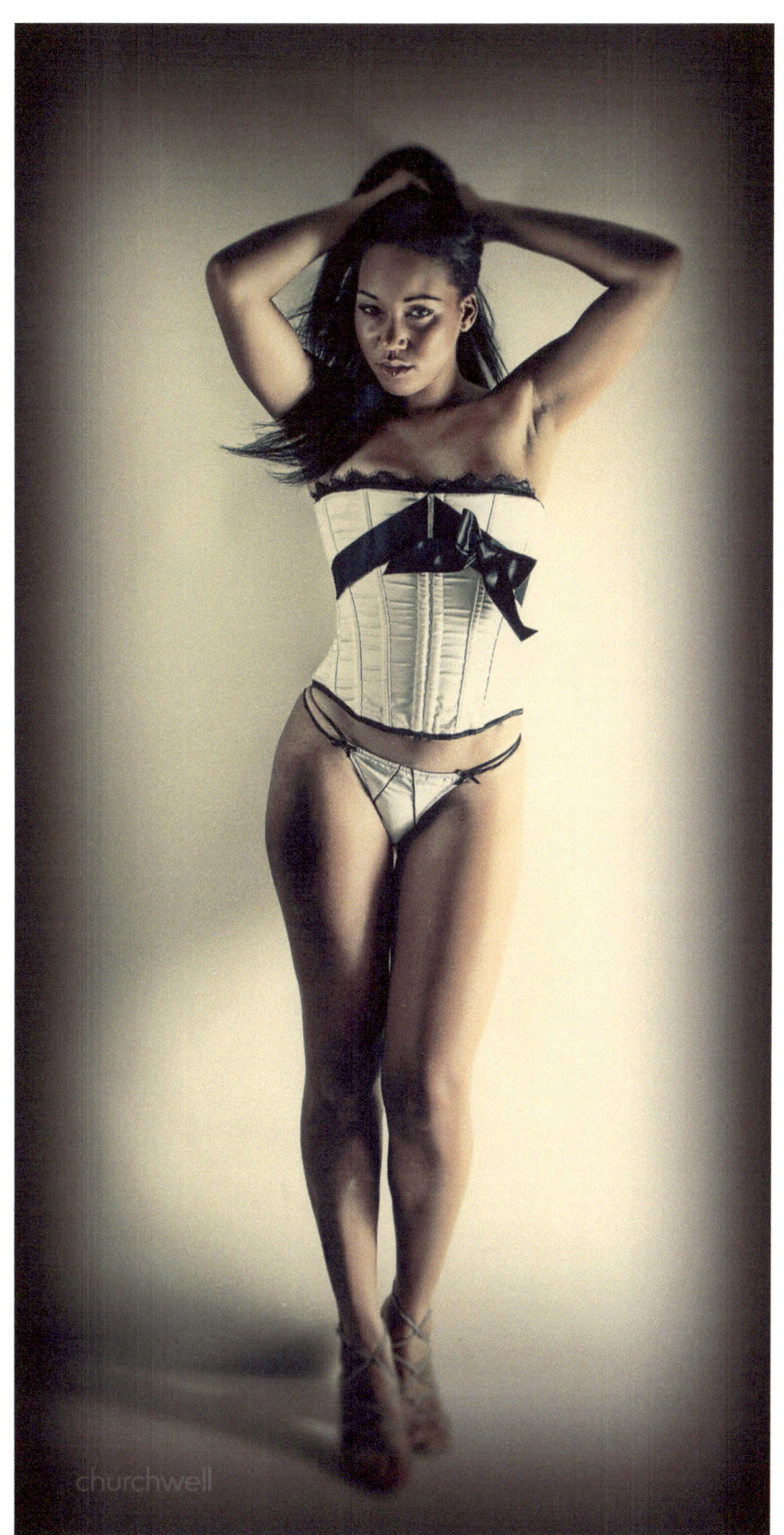

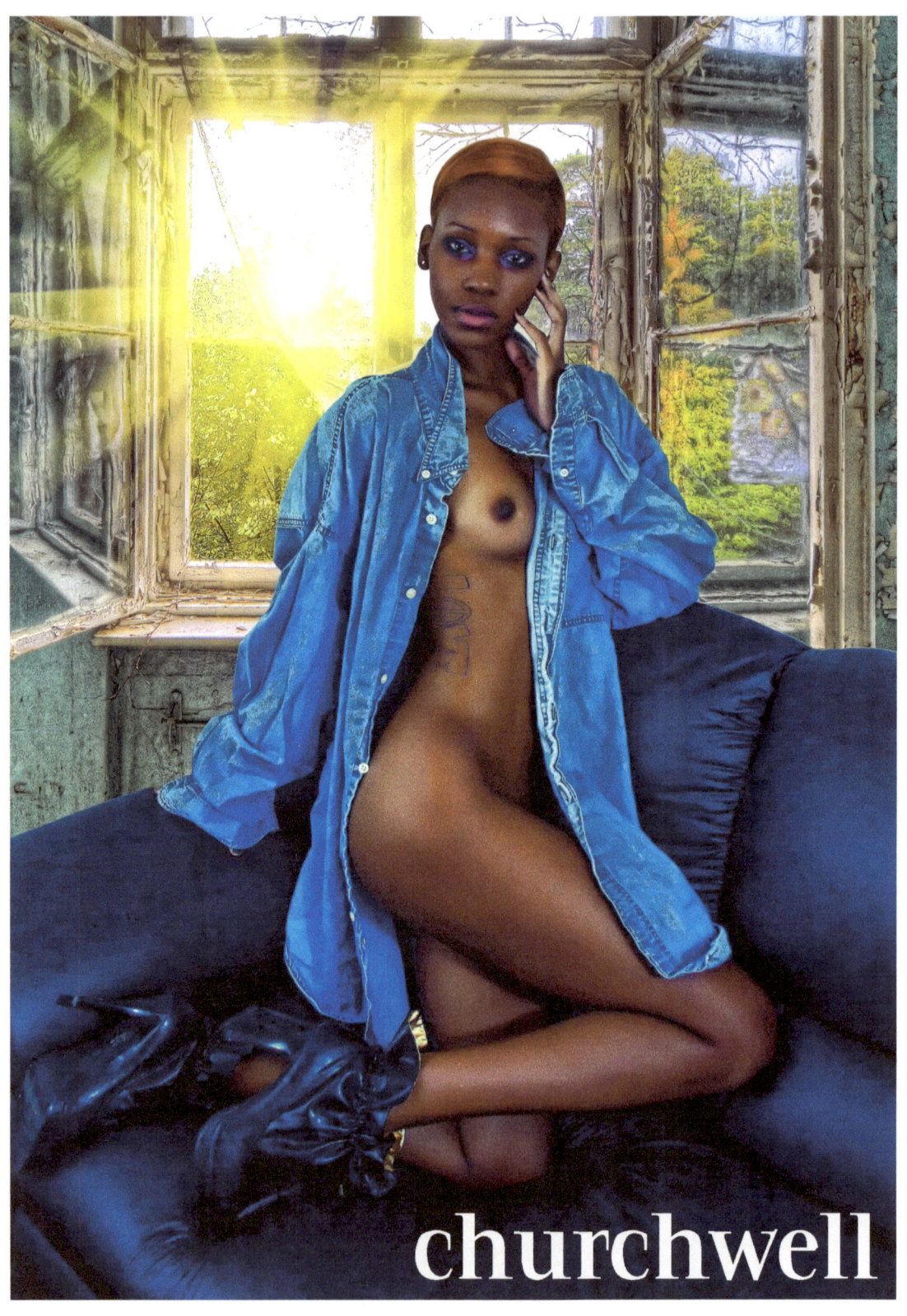

churchwell

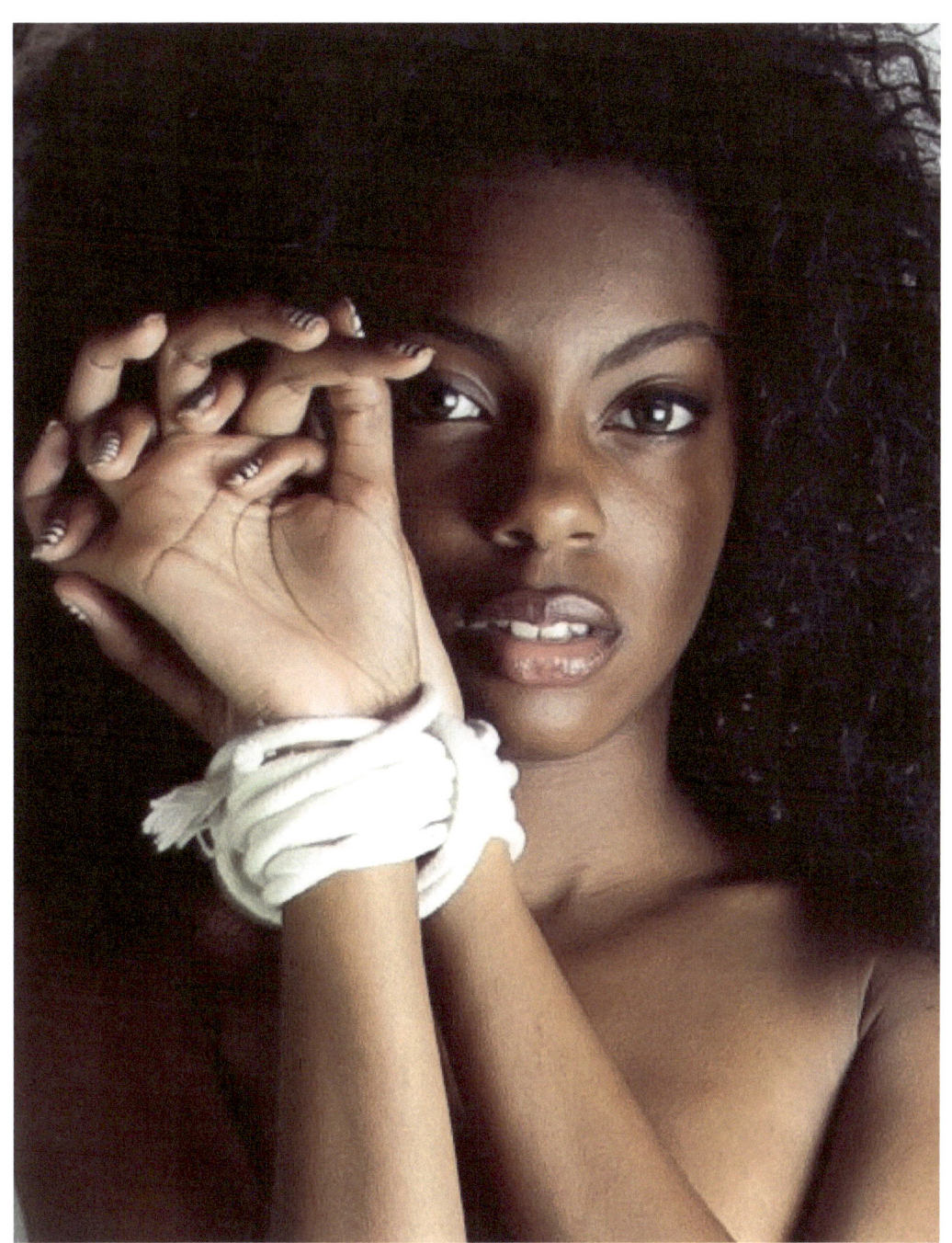

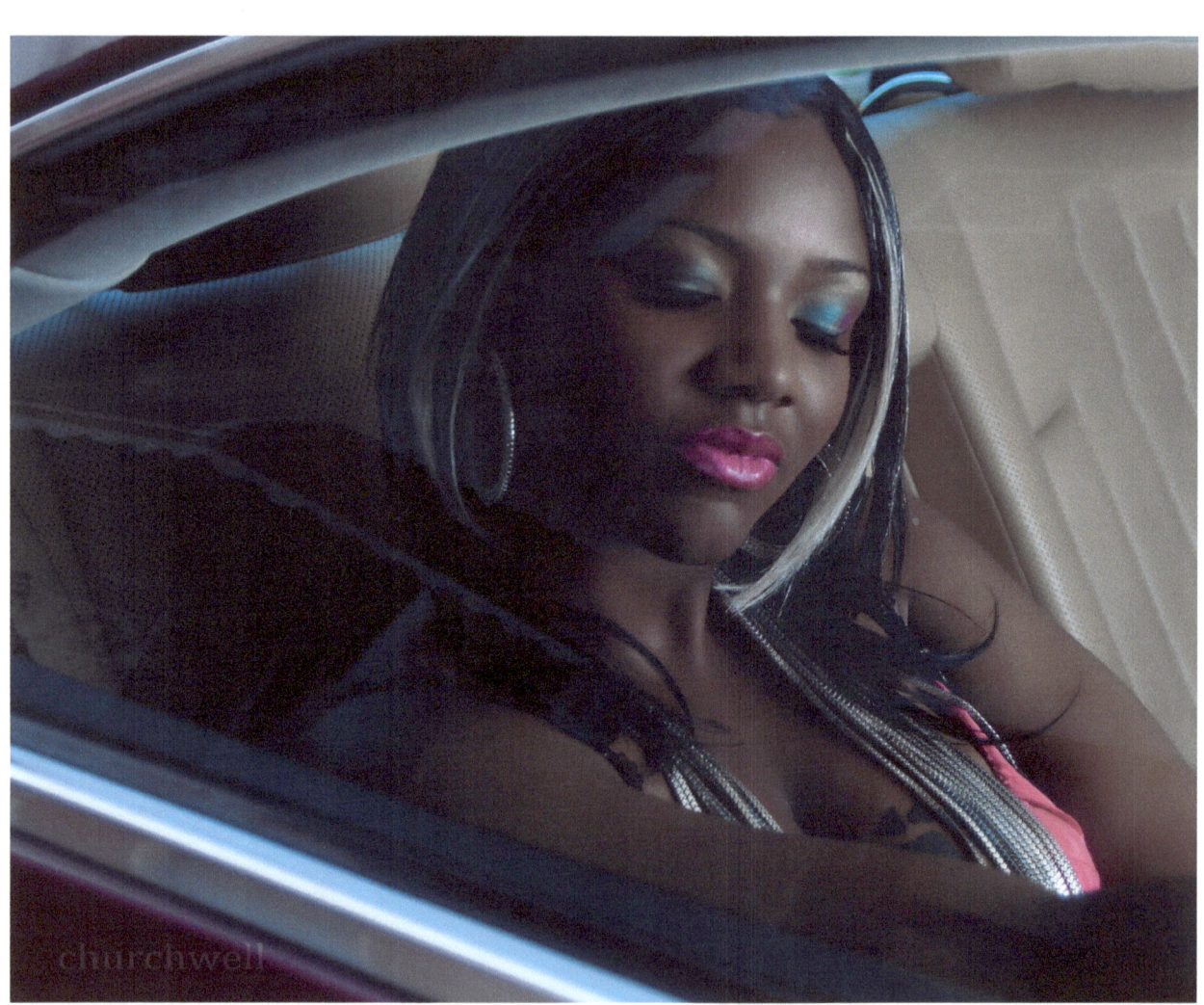

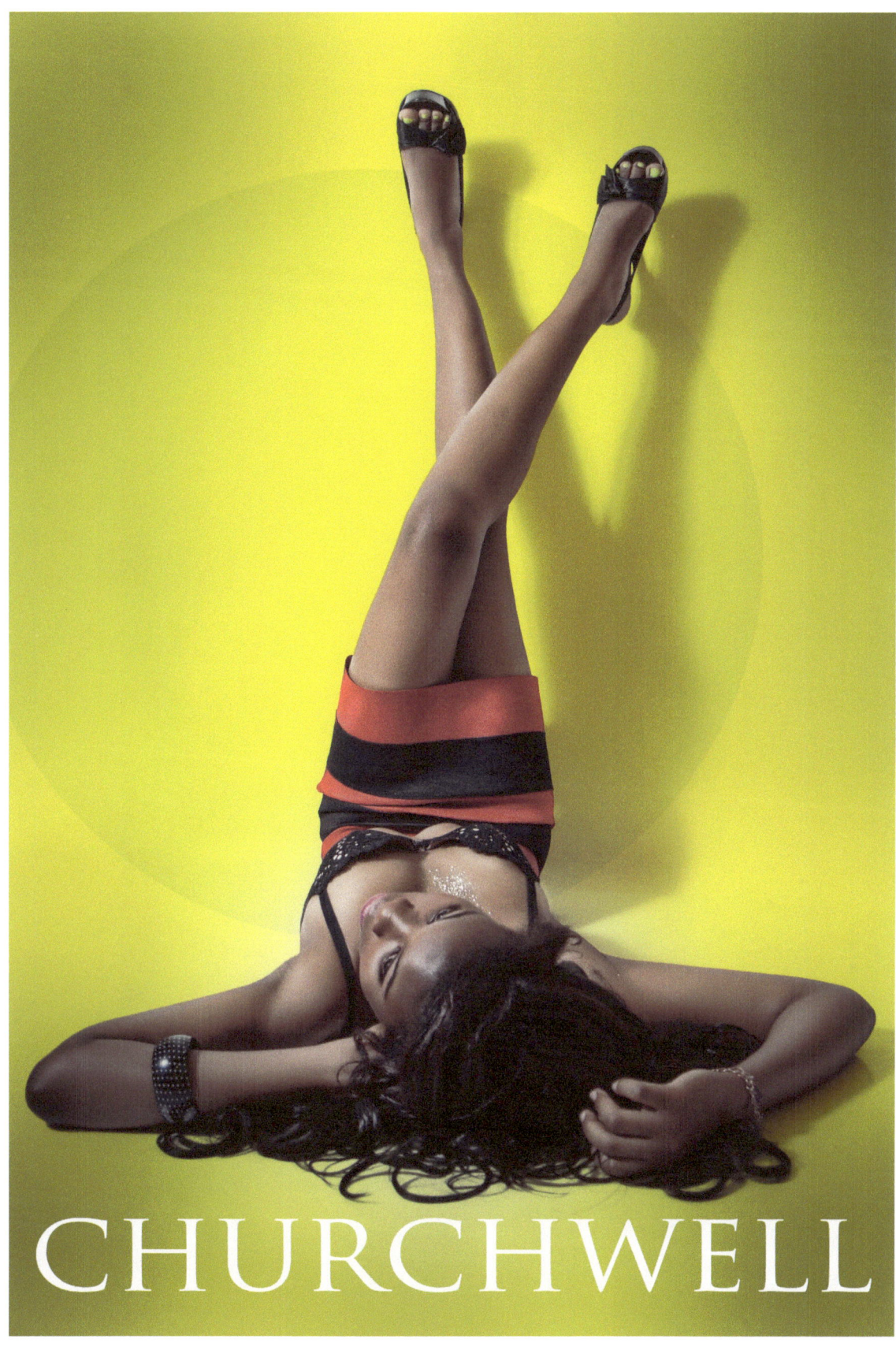

CHURCHWELL

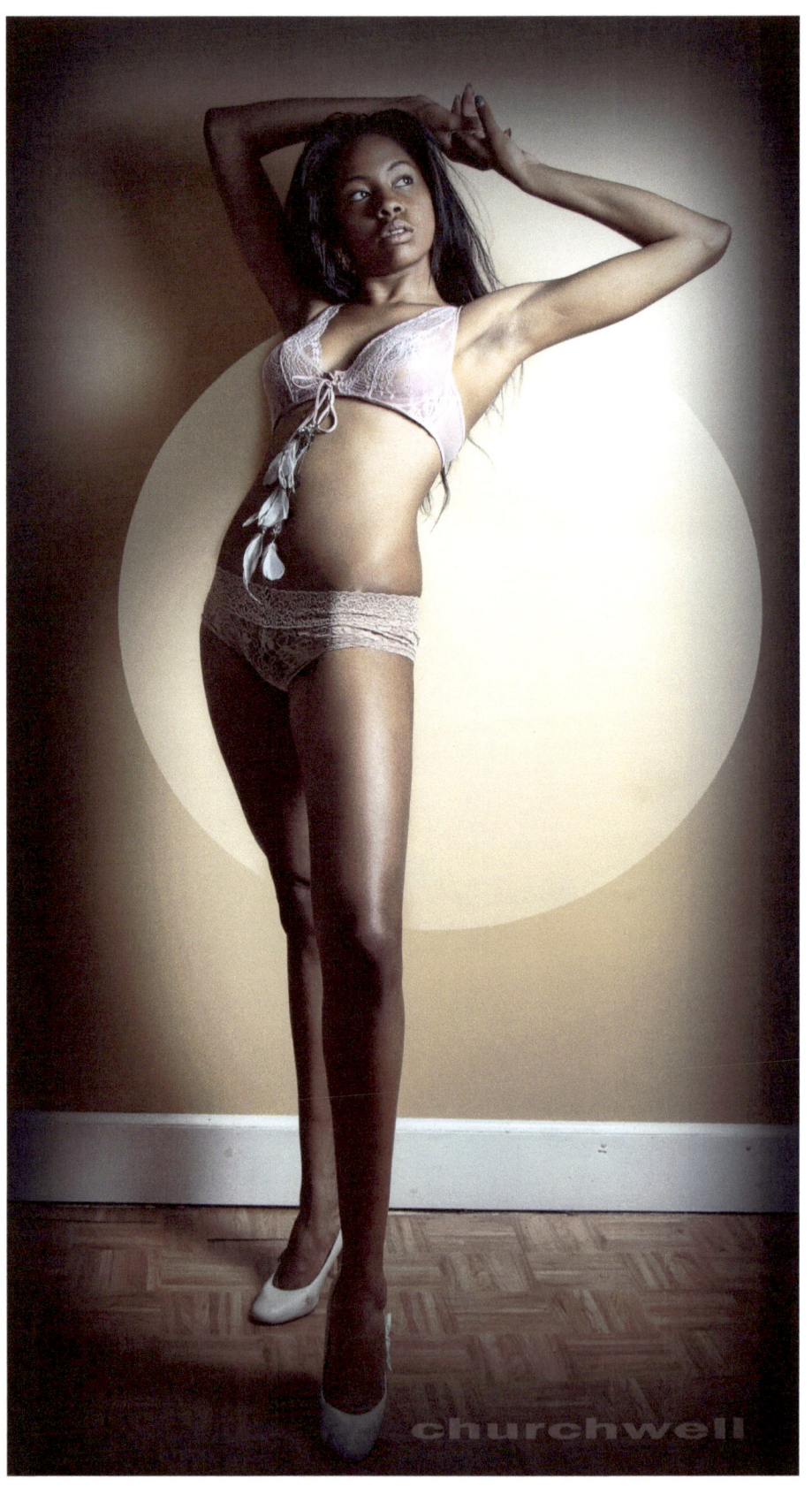

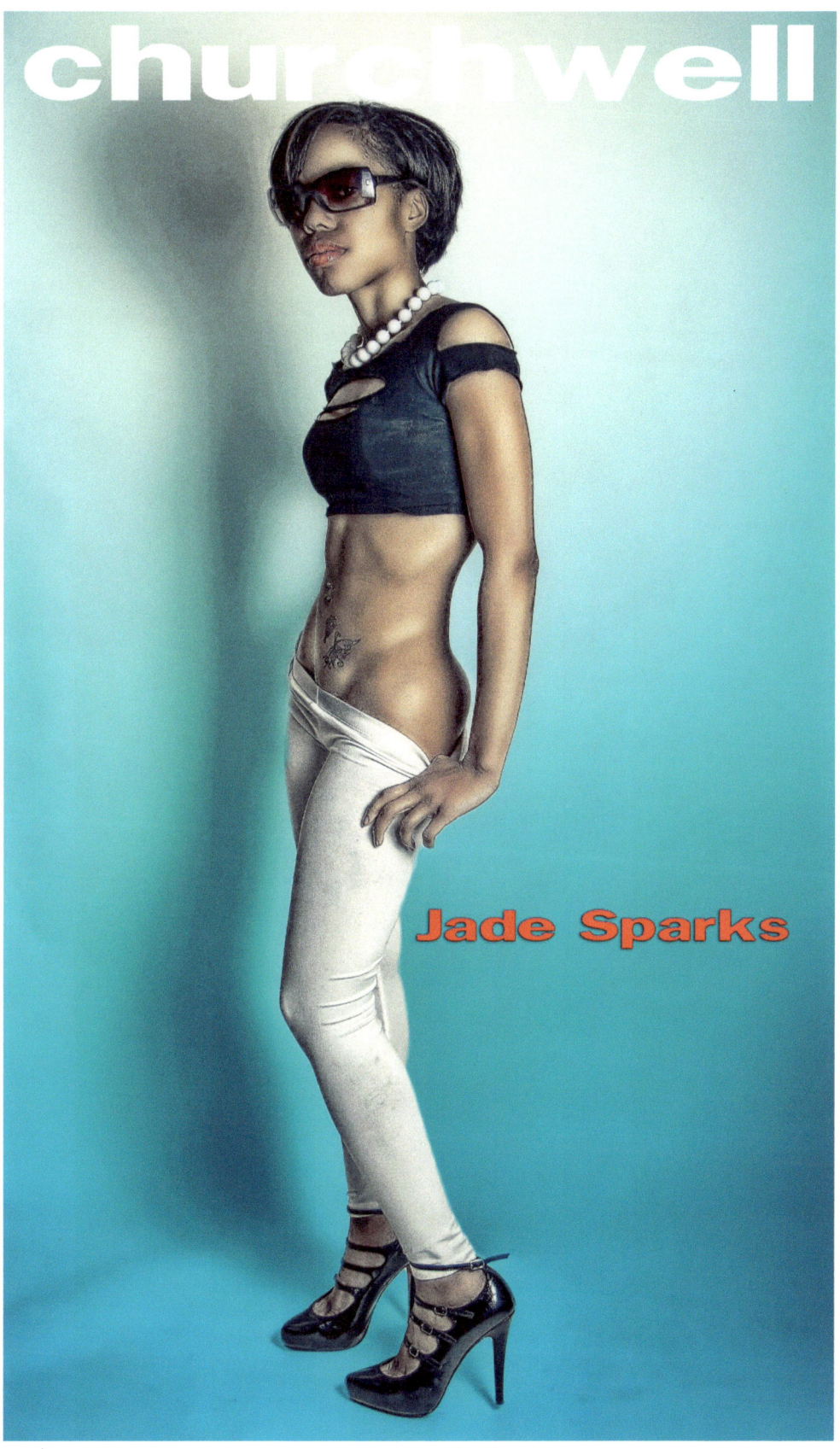

churchwell

Jade Sparks

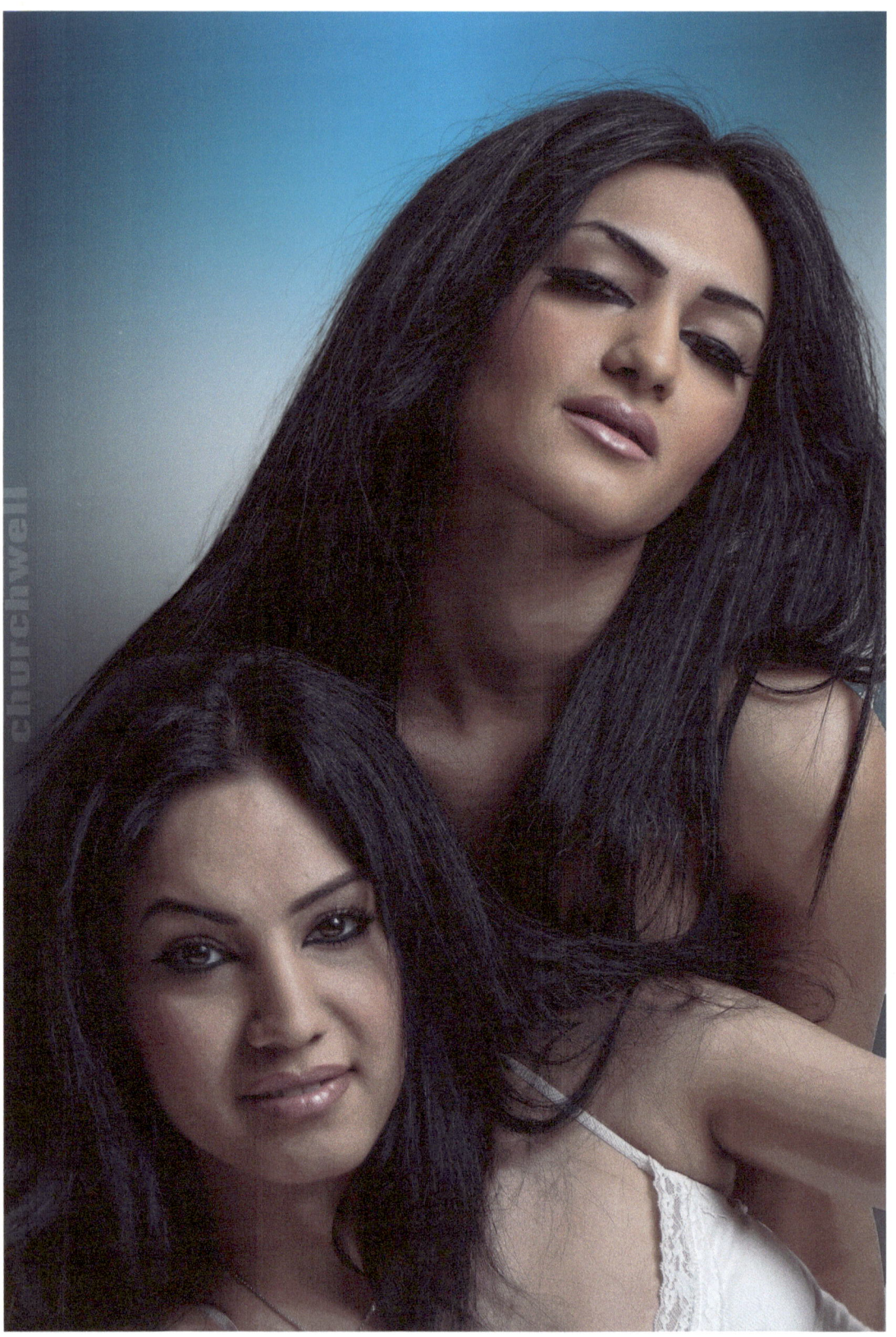

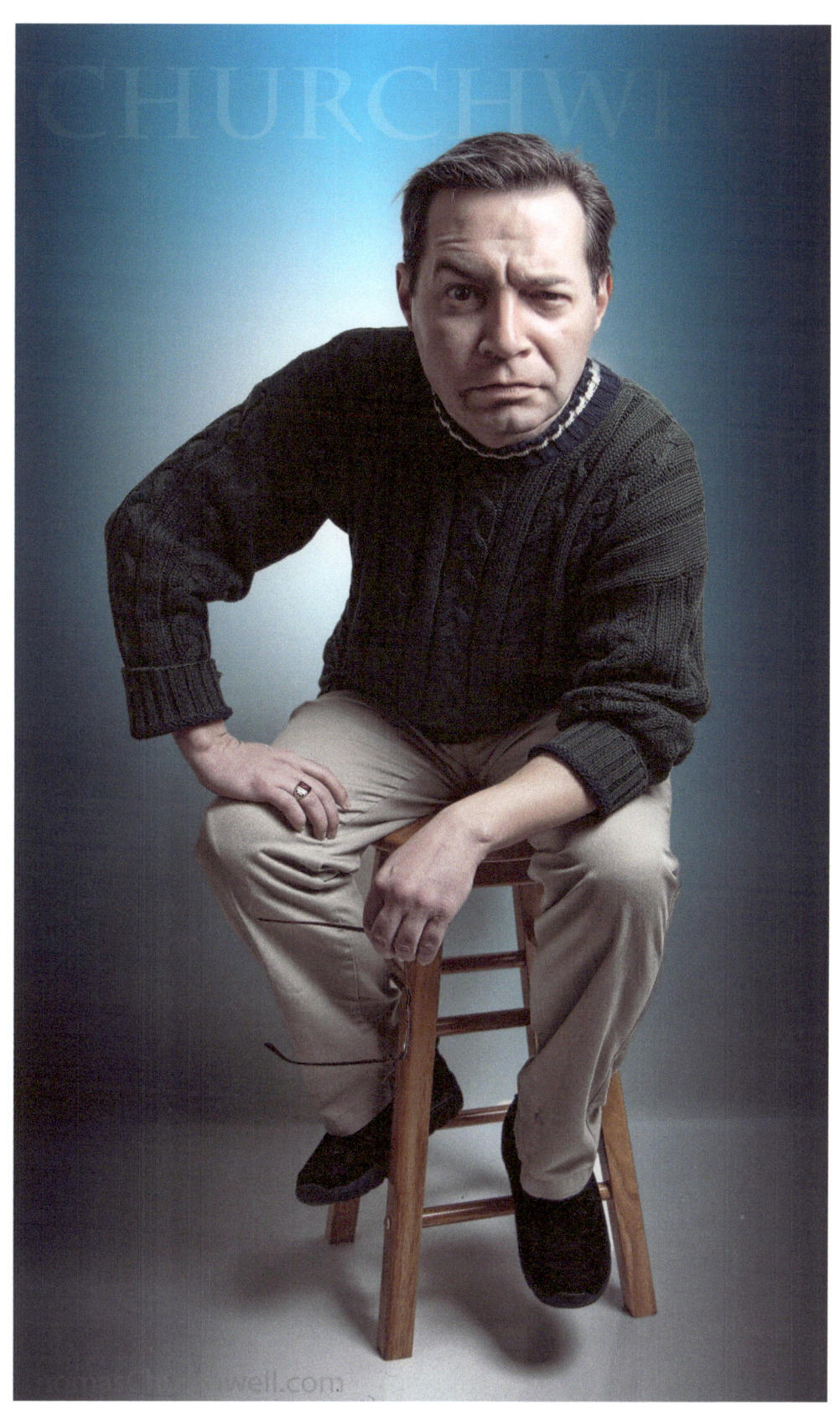

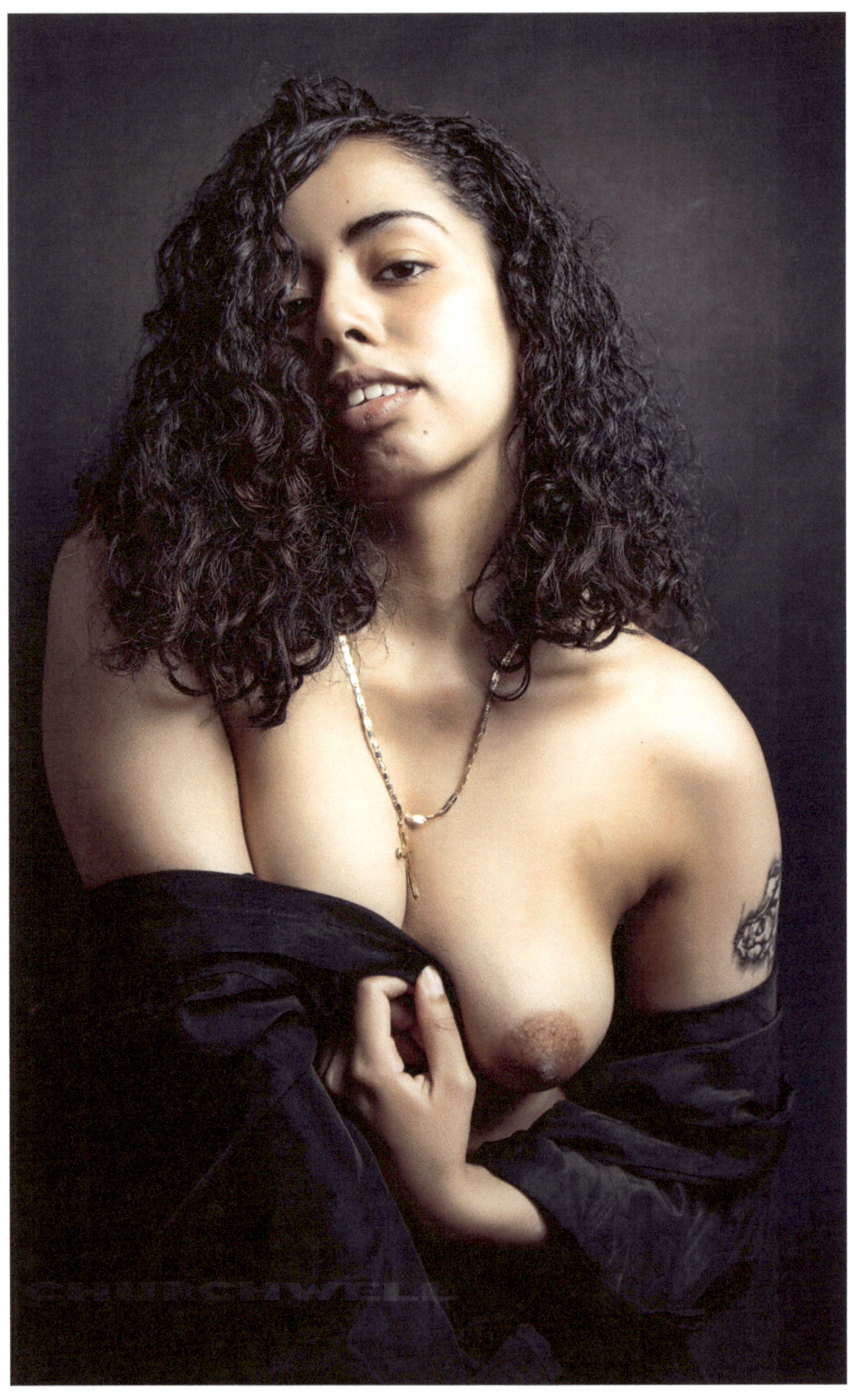

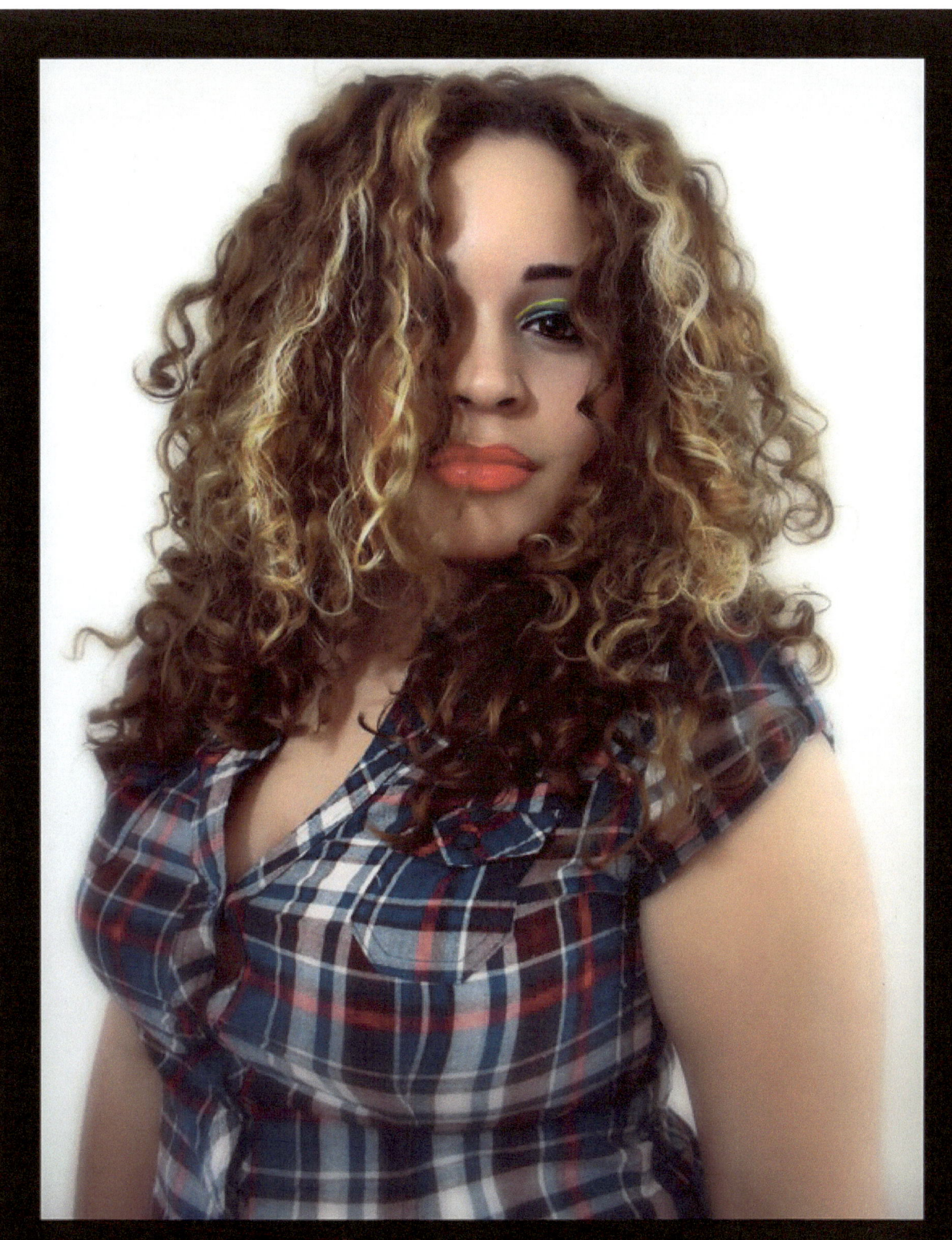

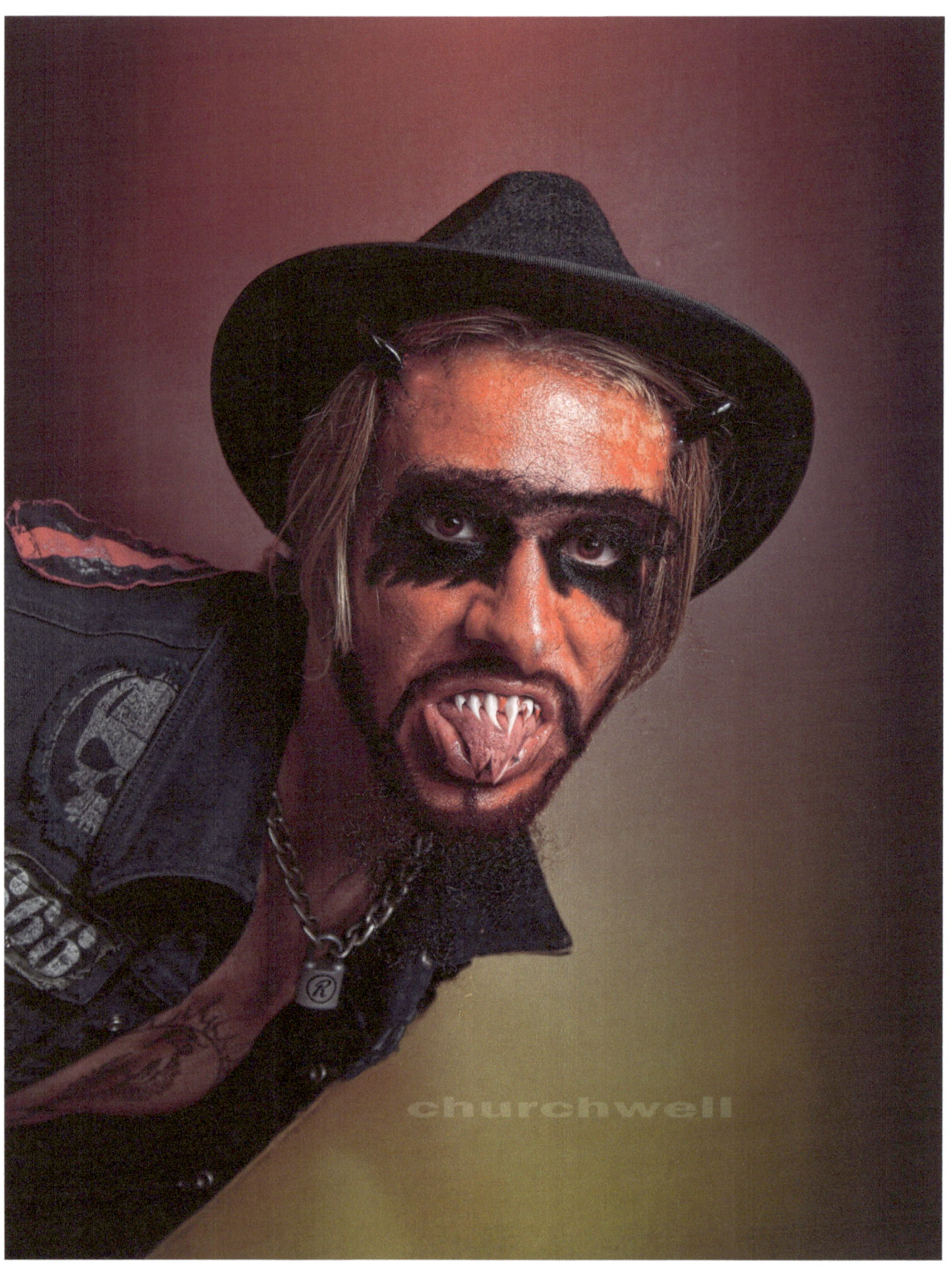

churchwell

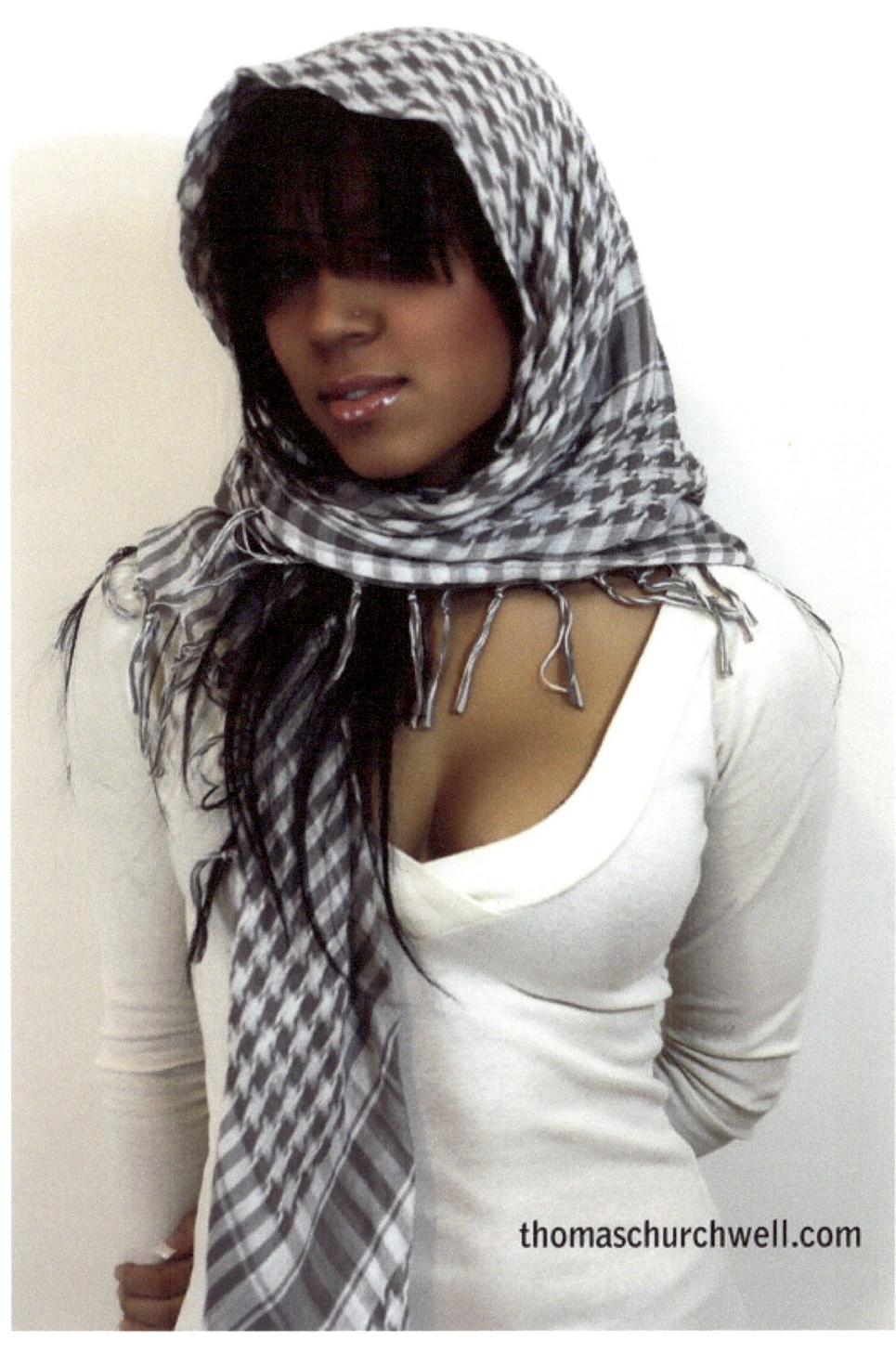

thomaschurchwell.com

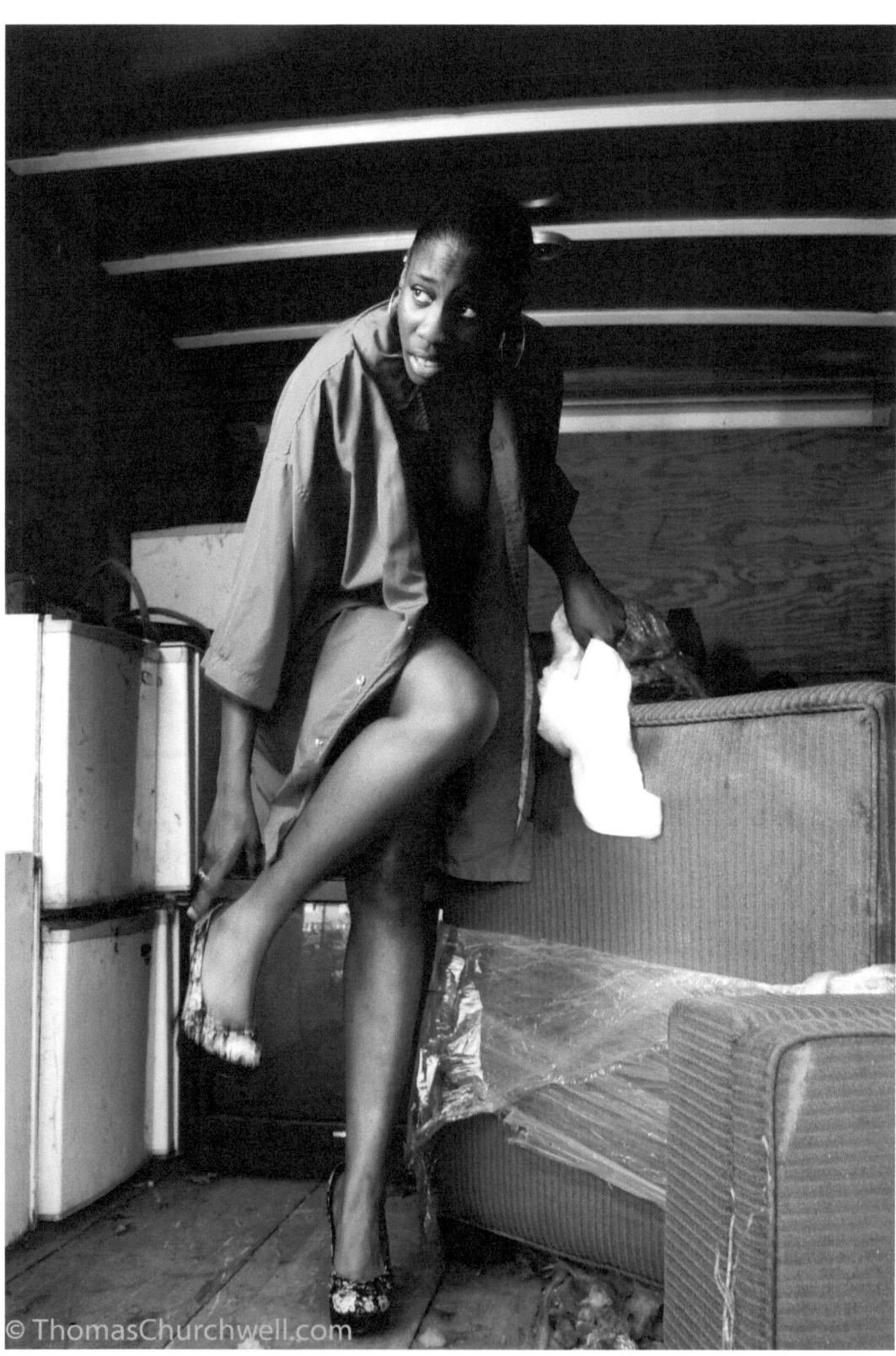

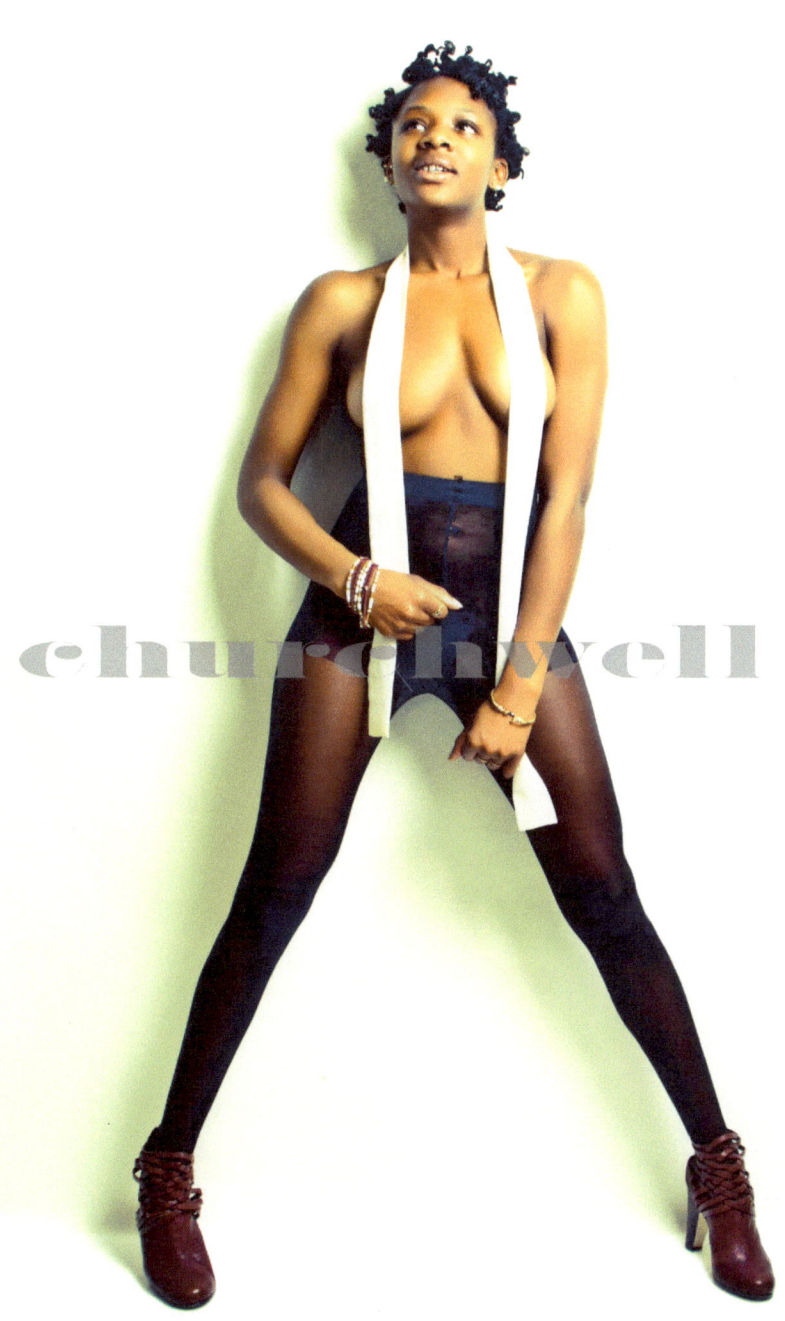

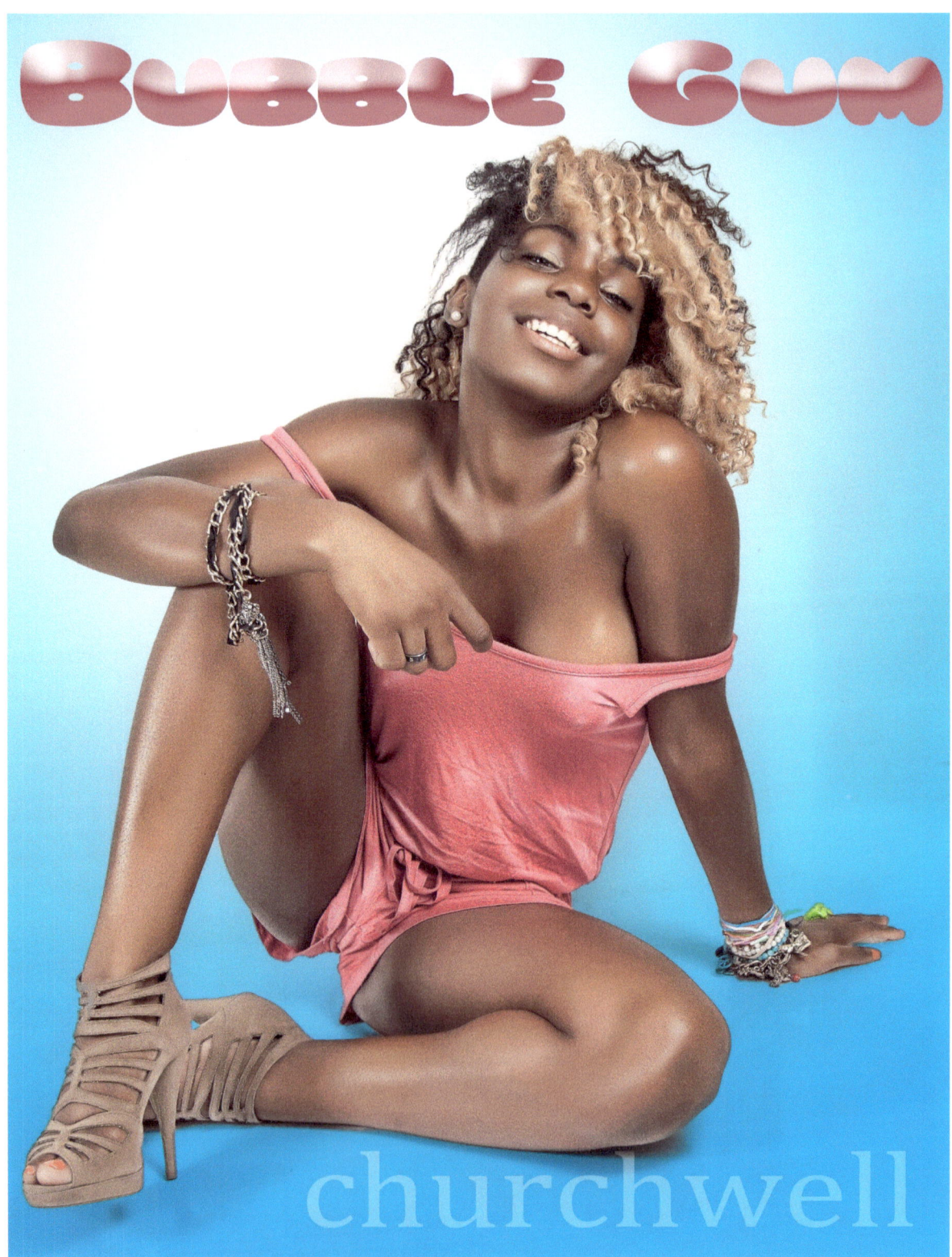

BUBBLE GUM

churchwell

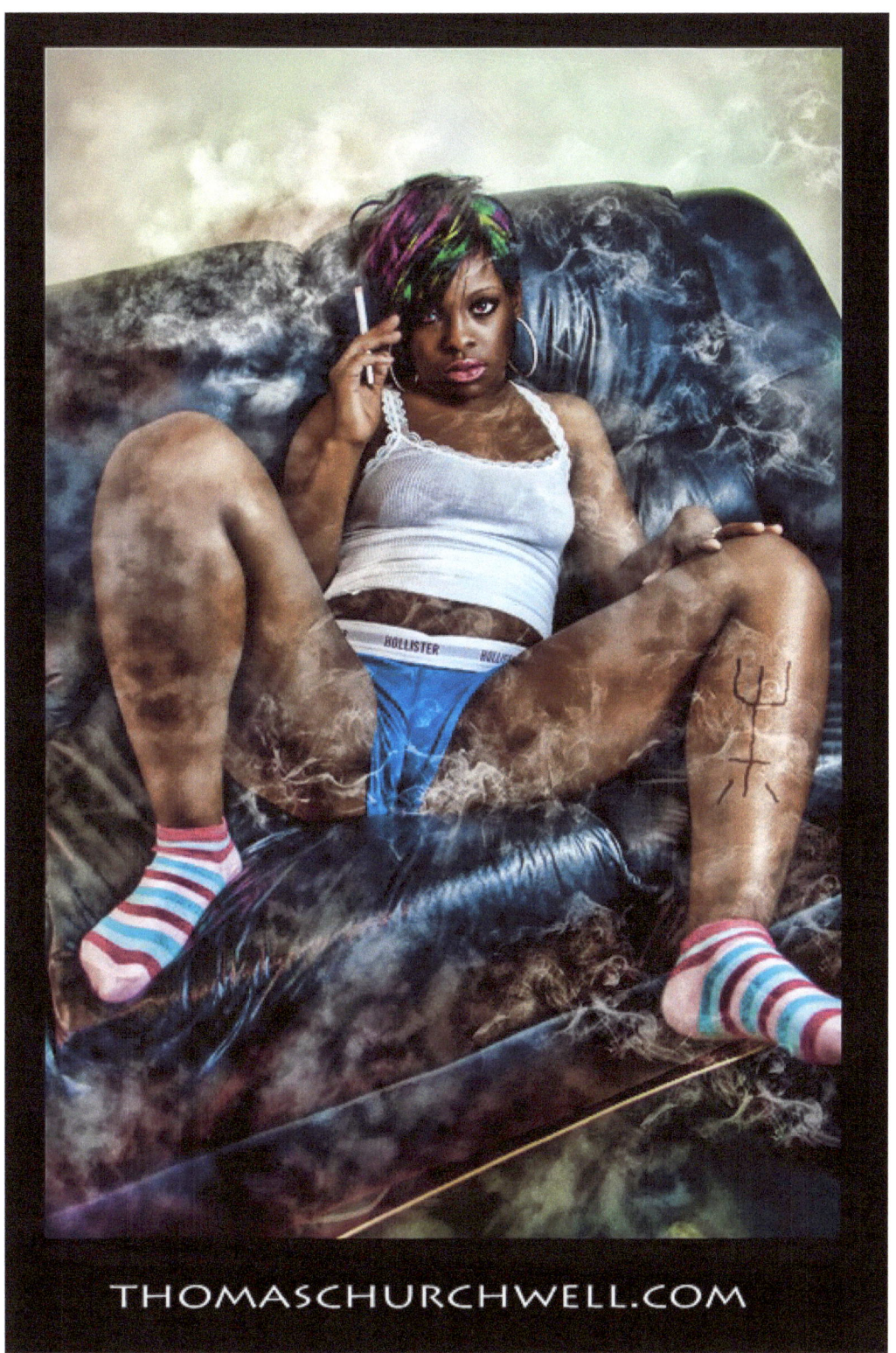

THOMASCHURCHWELL.COM

www.ingramcontent.com/pod-product-compliance
Lightning Source LLC
Chambersburg PA
CBHW041309180526
45172CB00003B/1033